Henry Dared to Live

Henry Dared to Live

Henry J. Seiler

iUniverse, Inc.

New York Bloomington Shanghai

Henry Dared to Live

iUniverse books may be ordered through booksellers or by contacting:

iUniverse
1663 Liberty Drive
Bloomington, IN 47403
www.iuniverse.com
1-800-Authors (1-800-288-4677)

ISBN: 978-0-595-47861-3 (pbk)
ISBN: 978-0-595-71499-5 (cloth)

Printed in the United States of America

This book is dedicated to my parents,
my sister,
and my extended family and friends.

Contents

Heaven's Very Special Child

A meeting was held quite far from earth.
"It's time again for another birth."
Said the angels to the Lord above.
"This special child will need much love.
His progress may seem very slow,
Accomplishments he may not show
And he'll require extra care
From the folks he meets way down there.
He may not run or laugh or play,
His thoughts may seem quite far away.
In many ways he won't adapt.
And he'll be known as handicapped.
So let's be careful where he's sent.
We want his life to be content.
Please, Lord, find parents who
Will do a special job for you.
They will not realize right away
The leading role they're asked to play,
But with this child sent from above
Comes stronger faith and richer love.
And soon they'll know the privilege given
In caring for this gift from heaven.

Their precious charge, so meek and mild,

Is heaven's very special child."

Author Unknown

Henry,

I got your manuscript yesterday and read it cover to cover. It was an amazing read. I remember bits and pieces of your story as the cousin who lived far away, but reading it in your own words was special. I cried, I smiled, I laughed, and I celebrated for you as I read it.

You are a gift and a blessing. It's certain that we have an impact on others, either positive or negative. You have affected many people in a very positive way (as you do today).

I hope that you get this published. This is a story with lessons for many people on many different levels. This is a story for the athlete, the friend, the child, the patient, the parent …

May God continue to bless you! You are a hero to me!

Love, your cousin,

Robin Winterfeldt

I am Henry Seiler.

This is my story, and it is about taking life as it comes to you; working through every day just as if it were like any other ordinary day. I want this book to give the reader hope and inspiration to handle life as it comes.

Prologue
The Quickest Trip

Henry was eleven years old, energetic and wiry. He was an athlete in the best sense of the term. He was bright eyed, eager to learn, and eager to please. The boy was a sponge in wrestling lessons—you just told him what to do on the mat once and he mastered it in the next one or two attempts.

He had one older sister, Sherri, and two younger sisters, Vicki and Cindi. They loved him like a brother—not lavishly but not distantly either. He loved them back. This close-knit family relationship was fostered and expected by their parents. They supported one another as much as two people could. Their Catholic upbringing allowed nothing less.

The OPTIMIST says we live in the best of all possible worlds; the pessimist fears this is true.

James Branch Cabell

On a bright May Wednesday after school, Henry was excited to give his wrestling mentor, Bob a gift—just a T-shirt, but Henry had bought the gift especially for him. This red T-shirt was special; it had "COACH" printed across the back in big blue capital letters. Bob was a high school student, about to graduate in a few months. Their age difference was not an issue—they both loved and excelled at their sport. The two were also close friends.

Bob arrived at Henry's house on a motorcycle belonging to his sister's boyfriend. He had never driven one before, but had been given the keys to "take it for a spin." Imagine Henry's excitement when Bob invited him, his little buddy, to hop on behind him and "hold on tight!"

After carefully testing its ability to hold the road, Bob headed the swift two-wheeler towards a not-so-heavily-traveled winding road. As they began down a sloping grade, the sand-sprinkled pavement caused some tire slippage. With Bob inexperienced on the throttle, the bike somersaulted over the curb just six feet from a telephone pole. The driver was flung to the left. Henry catapulted forward in an arc, encountering a guy-wire attached to the pole. After a moment of silence, Bob realized he was all right, but his little buddy lay in a tangled heap of limbs.

Rushing to him, fearing the worst, he scooped him up in his arms and clumsily trotted towards a nearby white house, gaining momentum and balance. He mustered up as much volume in his trembling voice as he could to scream, "Help!"

The little fellow lay in a hospital bed, in intensive care, in a coma. His parents were at the foot of the bed, where one or the other or both had been for the last forty-three days. At the bed was his wrestling coach, Mr. Kremer, dear to the family and especially close to this eleven-year-old wrestling prodigy.

Mr. Kremer, as others, had been encouraged to speak to the boy and to use as much sensory language as possible. He held each of Henry's hands in his hands as he spoke.

Henry's hands squeezed the coach's hands, and his forearms became tense. Mr. Kremer jerked in astonishment. Henry's parents jumped to their feet!

Henry might just make it! The room resounded with the deafening scream of, "YES! He IS going to make it! He lives!"

After wrinkle-browed, head-wagging negativity by the doctors, the arduous therapy began. Its triumphs were remedial. The medical experts continuously cautioned the family against hopes of any recovery, much less a prompt one.

Here begins the exhilarating success story of an athlete's determination to win. His opponent wasn't on the mat. There was no whistle to start this match—just stiff-willed, obstinate pursuit of a self-set goal. This is also a testimony to a family's relentless, constant support. This is about tough love and the response to it. This is the story of Henry Seiler, a stubborn youth who knew what he wanted. This is about the family that backed him, the friends that changed, and the victory he won! This is the story of how Henry dared to live.

Keep your goal always in your mind. Keep an eye on your goal. Never let up on your goal. If you want something badly enough, that goal is yours. But you have to relentlessly pursue the goal!

1

The Beginning

Hearing Henry tell his story, one might think there had been a black cloud over his head since conception. This is not how Henry views his life.

Henry's father is known as Hank. Hank's hometown was St. Benedict, Iowa. Hank served in the army for two years during the Korean War. On November 25, 1960, Hank Seiler married Berniece Smith. Hank worked as a hog buyer for Decker's Buying Station. Berniece grew up in Algona, Iowa. During the first few years of their marriage, Berniece worked as a butcher for Hood's Grocery.

Berniece had a difficult labor with their second child. On December 21, 1963, he was born breech and deprived of oxygen. This resulted in the baby's nose being pushed up to his forehead, causing convulsions. Hank really wanted a son. Berniece did not want the doctor to tell Hank whether they had a girl or a boy. When the doctor talked to Hank he said, "I am not to tell you whether you have a son or a daughter," this ruined the surprise. Hank knew he had a son.

Three days later, Christmas Eve, Hank and Berniece headed home with their newborn son. This was an interesting scene. Hank pulled up to the Kossuth County Hospital in his '54 Plymouth. He jumped out to help his wife into the car. Before anyone could make a move, Great Grandma Mary slipped into the front seat and insisted on holding the baby. Berniece settled into the backseat. As the family was driving home, Berniece asked Hank, "What should we name our son?" Great Grandma Mary replied, "His name is Henry Joseph

Seiler the Third." This was the beginning of Henry's challenging yet fulfilling journey.

On Christmas Day, the Seiler family stayed snuggled in their little apartment on Watertower Street in Algona, Iowa. The day started out as any other Christmas Day. The family exchanged presents and enjoyed the gift of Henry. Before long, the small apartment was swarming with forty friends and relatives who wanted to meet Henry.

What we share with our children is what will be in their hearts.

When Henry was born he had a bad ear infection. They didn't have medicine like they have now. This ear infection resulted in hearing loss, which lasted one year. To complicate things, when Henry was three and a half months old, he had several convulsions, a defect relating to his breech birth as determined by Dr. Rooney at Kossuth County Hospital. Henry was diagnosed with idiopathic convulsive disorder. He had six seizures that lasted no longer than a minute each. Henry would have to take medication for the next five years, a long time for such a little guy. It was even longer for a mom and dad who had to administer the medication daily. God bless them. They stuck by Henry through it all! While there may be parents who don't care that much for their children and subject their children to neglect and abuse or simply don't give enough of themselves to stand by their kids through tough times, Henry's parents stood by him.

Awesome:

Stiff-willed, obstinate pursuit of a self-set goal!

As a four-year-old, Henry was inquisitive, as most children are. As a result, he broke his nose twice by the age of five. Later, Henry would not remember his first broken nose, but he heard the story so often that he painted a picture in his mind of what had happened. Henry had a toy that he called a "scooter horse." It was a little brown and tan hobbyhorse. It had a little horse's head on the end of a three-foot piece of doweling. One day, Henry rode his scooter horse down the basement steps and lost his footing. He took a somersault and tumbled down the last few steps, breaking his nose.

The other time Henry broke his nose, he was pushing bricks around as if they were little bulldozers on a slight hill of dirt mixed with gravel. There were also some pieces of rubble in that pile—small cement chunks that ended up in the pile of dirt when a cement floor was poured. Henry pushed a brick over the top of the pile. As he reached the summit of this modest hill, Henry lost his balance and smacked into the brick wall. The impact broke both his nose and the brick he hit.

These events took place in Mason City, Iowa. In 1973, the Seilers moved to Marshalltown, Iowa. Henry was about nine years old and in the third grade.

Henry's family had a strong belief in Catholicism. He was an altar boy and enjoyed assisting the priest during mass. Henry's memories of his parish priest, Father Norton, were that of a gentle, holy man. Father Norton was a great priest. He taught Henry to be an altar boy and Father Norton enjoyed seeing the Seiler family on Sundays and Holy days. The family had great respect for their priest.

Two years went by without Henry taking any tumbles that resulted in broken bones—not even his nose!

What we share with our children is what will be in their hearts.

2

Learning the Ropes

In 1975, Henry became interested in wrestling. Wrestling involves enormous discipline. Wrestlers must have a toned body, agile reflexes, and a strategic mind. Henry was not afraid of the grueling workouts or the intense practices. He was a talented boy who quickly learned the basics and was soon competing at collegiate, or folkstyle, wrestling. Henry was a natural.

Henry was a member of the Marshalltown Wrestling Club. The directors and coaches were Mike Kremer, Larry Fox, Gary Hansen, and Tom Crandall. These upstanding individuals were responsible for starting the club and coaching the young wrestlers. The club was comprised of students in grades four through eight. Dennis Leavy, Mike Fox, and Henry's parents were members of the board of directors.

The Marshalltown Wrestling Club completed their season with success. The club members participated in eight meets, wrestling 981 matches. The club's record for the season was 671 wins and 310 losses, resulting in a 69 percent winning record. For the season, the Marshalltown Wrestling Club had forty-three first-place, forty-seven second-place, twenty-nine third-place, and three fourth-place match results. Out of the one hundred club members, seventy-four went to tournaments and fifty-five placed in the top four at least once.

Henry's participation in the Marshalltown Wrestling Club allowed his natural talent in wrestling to shine through. Henry's talents and wrestling abilities were attracting the attention of wrestling greats such as Dan Gable, an Olympic gold medalist. Dan has been referred to as "the greatest wrestler in U.S. history," a humble person who "does not seek excellence to be honored" but who "honors us all by seeking excellence" (*Des Moines Sunday Register*, September 11, 1983).

At the age of eleven, soon after the recognition by Dan Gable, Henry became a member of the AAU (Amateur Athletic Union) Junior Olympic Freestyle Wrestling Team. Henry successfully wrestled in a tournament against the Mexican Federation Team. Freestyle, a much quicker-paced form of wrestling, was foreign to the young wrestlers of the Marshalltown Wrestling Club. Talking with his teammates, Henry would compare folkstyle to socialism and freestyle to capitalism. Socialism is a political and economic theory that advocates for the equality of opportunity for all members of the community. Capitalism is an economic system in which the means of production, distribution, and exchange are privately owned and operated for private profit. This was a great comparison, for folkstyle wrestling has an emphasis on teamwork while freestyle is focused on individual performance. The Marshalltown wrestlers needed to learn a new style of wrestling in order to compete at the AAU level. These boys had only one month to learn freestyle wrestling and to hone their skills.

Bob Logan was a coach and mentor for these young wrestlers. Bob had a makeshift wrestling room set up in his basement. The wrestlers that were to compete in the AAU Junior Olympic Tournament met in Bob's basement daily. This was a challenging time for the boys, as they learned the rules and moves associated with freestyle wrestling.

At the end of these practices, the boys would nurse fatigued and sore muscles, but their endurance paid off. The U.S. team quickly discovered that they could win at freestyle tournaments. In fact, this team ended up winning the AAU Tournament of Freestyle Wrestling in Cedar Falls, Iowa.

Mike Fox and Dennis Leavy were also talented wrestlers that made the AAU tournament. Both went on to have successful high school wrestling careers. Greg Kearney, the son of Lou Kearney, was in the upper weight class at the AAU tournament.

During his seventh-grade school year, Bob Logan excelled in wrestling. Success didn't come immediately, however, and Bob sometimes shirked practice in the early days. One day, Bob's friends taped him up from head to toe with athletic tape and carried him to practice. After this event, Bob no longer tried to avoid practice. Bob Logan went on to win the state title during his senior year of high school, elating his coaches from junior high and high school wrestling.

Awesome:
Stiff-willed, obstinate pursuit of a self-set goal!

3

Henry's Story Begins

Bob lived in Marshalltown. Bob was a blond-haired, light-skinned young man with freckles on his light-haired arms and on hairless cheeks. He had an almost rosy complexion. He was like a brother to Henry. Even though he was eight years older than Henry, he was like a part of the family. Henry had great respect for him. Bob spoke meaningful words. He talked about being in shape and about wrestling, and Henry knew he meant what he was saying. Bob was always friendly, happy, and sincere. You could say he was a good role model. You could count on him to shoot straight and still be friendly. He was like a part of Henry.

Bob knew what Henry was like. He was a great trainer, too. He would work with Henry to make him a better wrestler. He was at the Seilers' house a lot. When Hank realized Henry was good at wrestling, he set up a place to work out in the basement. Hank wanted Bob to be Henry's mentor, and he agreed without any discussion. Bob was a freestyle wrestler, a really good one. He had won plenty of tournaments in high school and was the coach's right hand man.

Bob was a good coach: he knew what Henry would do next no matter how hard Henry tried to fool him. For example, when Bob was sparring against Henry, Henry would try doing something a little different from what Bob had instructed him to do. Bob was right on top of it, getting the better of Henry to prove that his advice was the best advice, no matter what.

Bob was always like that. He would evaluate the moves Henry was making while practicing, then point out a better, swifter, more cunning way to outmaneuver the opponent, and he would always be right. His instruction helped Henry to become such a good wrestler.

In 1975, a group of Marshalltown boys were given an opportunity to wrestle. Bob was one of the coaches. A team was assembled, and after a month of consistent practice, the boys had adopted freestyle wrestling. With just one month's preparation, the AAU team whooped the other Mexican Federation Team, and Bob was the biggest reason for their impressive wins.

Bob instilled something in Henry that never went away. He would say, "We should envision winning, and keep that idea in the back of our minds throughout every match. Not just our individual matches, but the whole meet." The team was to treat the whole tournament as if it were an individual match-up. This helped instill in the team a sense of sportsmanship that turned them into a wrestling "machine."

As Henry grew up, he whittled away on that concept, honing it until it was constantly in his thoughts. He eventually boiled it down to an important constant in his life: "Keep your goal always in your mind. Keep an eye on your goal. Never let up on your goal. If you want something badly enough, that goal is yours. But you have to relentlessly pursue it."

Henry really looked up to Bob. He loved him as one loves a father or a favorite uncle. Henry would do anything for Bob, and Bob would do anything for Henry. Bob enjoyed being around Henry.

Henry wanted to let Bob know that he thought he was the greatest guy in his world, so in early 1975—it might have been February or March—Henry bought Bob a shirt that said "COACH" across the back.

Henry had learned the meaning of acknowledgment from his dad. Hank instilled in his children the values of appreciation, understanding, and honesty. The Seiler children learned these values by the numerous acts of kindness demonstrated by their parents. As mentioned earlier, Hank had redone the basement of their house so the boys could work out down there. There were mats to wrestle on and places to sit and watch. There were milk jugs with sand in them for the boys to lift to build up their muscles. Bob and Hank made sure they were exercising the right way.

The Marshalltown Wrestling Association was the first of its kind in Marshalltown. Henry's parents were the president and copresident. They had weekly meetings, and every week they would give the Traveling Trophy to the wrestler who was most energetic. Henry was the first recipient of the Traveling Trophy.

We should envision winning, and keep that idea in the back of our minds throughout every match. Not just the matches we did individually, but through the whole meet.

4

The Quickest Trip

Henry doesn't remember much about what happened just before the accident, but on May 7, 1975, he and Bob were in a motorcycle wreck.

That day Bob wore blue jeans that looked as if they just came out of the store: dark, dark blue denim with a leather patch that was almost hidden by his wide brown leather belt. The belt buckle was a brownish metal, almost brass colored. He wore a button-front blue and white plaid shirt. Its white buttons were not fastened, showing a clean white crewneck T-shirt. The tails of his shirt hung outside his jeans. Instead of loafers or sneakers, Bob wore high-topped work shoes, the kind with "lace catchers" instead of eyelets at the top.

Bob was straddling the gas tank of the shiny black motorcycle belonging to his older sister's boyfriend who had lent it to him. The boyfriend had come over to her house to visit and flirt a little. As they were talking out back by the garage, Bob happened to come out of the house and saw them talking. Playing devil's advocate, he engaged in some "brotherly" conversation. The boyfriend realized that this conversation was getting him off track, so he steered the conversation to his new motorcycle.

It worked! Bob could ogle with the best of them, and he realized what fun such a bike could be. Recognizing the opportunity to get Bob to quit bugging him, the boyfriend pitched the keys to Bob and invited him to take his new motorcycle for a spin.

Without much hesitation, Bob asked the necessary questions: "Do I need to choke it to get it started? What about the front brake: do I need to use it, or can I just use the rear brake?" And after very little coaxing, Bob's sister and her boyfriend were soon forgotten.

Off to Henry's house he went, gliding out of his driveway and onto the cobblestone street. He almost floated around the corner of Thirteenth Street and State. Within one breath, he glided up to the front of Henry's house.

Cutting the motor, Bob got his left shoe on the ground, swung his right back over the pliable, long black seat cushion, and stood next to the bike, balancing it there. Snapping the kickstand down with his right foot, he let the handlebar seek its own place and grinned at his admiring audience of Seiler kids and neighbors.

"Whoa!" Henry exclaimed in awe. "That can't be yours!"

"Nah, not hardly," replied Bob.

Bob would never have been able to keep something like this from Henry. They knew each other too well, and a secret like this would have been a signal of mistrust. If there was one thing the two friends held dear, it was their total trust of each other. There's no way they wouldn't have shared such a good—no, great—stroke of luck. This was fantastic! Almost too much to take in all at one time.

Bob talked excitedly to Henry and Ty (Henry's friend), trying to decide who would be honored with the first ride on the motorcycle. Bob made a decision: "Henry, little buddy, hop on and hold tight!" Henry was enthralled.

The emotions of being specially chosen raced through his eleven-year-old mind: pride at how he was being looked up to by his three sisters, that boyish excitement of new adventure, self-esteem of being the first to do this, surprise and a little bit of fear of the unknown. Henry had never been this close to a motorcycle, much less on one!

Bob headed towards Summit Street. Once at the Veterans home, heading east, he approached a rough winding road.

The pair was just cruising, feeling the power when needed. They enjoyed the wind in their hair. They were grinning and having to lick the fronts of their teeth. The warmish-cool May breeze turned often to a gusty wind.

As they begin down a sloping grade, Bob took his eyes off the variegated hard surface. He pointed silently to a gap in the distant trees off to the left. The front tire skated, the bike responding to Bob's aligning maneuver. Abruptly, the motorcycle slipped on the sand-sprinkled pavement and with a bit of inexperienced throttle, the bike somersaulted over the curb. The driver was flung to the left. Henry catapulted forward in an arc and encountered a guy-wire attached to a nearby telephone pole.

After a moment of silence, Bob woke up, shaken and disoriented but all right. He saw his little buddy lying in a tangled heap of limbs. Rushing to him, Bob saw no blood, but he scooped Henry up in his arms and clumsily trotted toward a nearby white house while gaining momentum and balance. He mustered as much volume in his trembling voice as he could to wail, "Help!" Bob thought Henry might have hit the gas tank before hurtling into the guy-wire.

Bob reached the closest house, which happened to be the commandant's home on the Iowa Veterans Home grounds. The commandant, Jack Dack, was eating his evening meal with his wife when the doorbell rang. Standing on the stoop was a young man with a child in his arms. The child appeared limp, his head flopped over to one side. Bob pleaded for help and Dack called the hospital emergency room. The local ambulance and emergency staff soon arrived at the commandant's home. Henry was placed in the ambulance and taken to the local hospital.

Henry's parents were not home at the time of the accident. Hank was at work and Berniece was at the Johnstons' house. This was a farm about seven miles south of Marshalltown.

Henry's sister Sherri, age thirteen, two years older than Henry, and his two younger sisters, Vicki, age nine, and Cindi, age eight, were at home when the call came through that there had been an accident. Sherri took the call. Mrs. Jack Dack told Sherri that they needed to contact Hank and Berniece immediately. Sherri gave Mrs. Dack the Johnstons' phone number. She knew that something terrible had happened. After Sherri hung up, she began to sob. The tears started to flow and they would not stop. As Sherri sat on the bottom step of the stairs, she was joined by her two younger sisters, Vicki and Cindi. They also started to cry. At this point, they had no information regarding the accident, but their hearts told them everything.

Ty had been waiting for Henry and Bob to return from their ride. Time went by and they did not return. Finally, Ty went home because it was time for dinner. As the family was eating their meal, they heard an ambulance go by with sirens blaring. Ty immediately knew that Henry and Bob had been in a motorcycle accident.

Mrs. Dack contacted Berniece at the Johnstons' farm, where they were cutting up beef for freezing. Berniece was told that Henry had been in a bike accident. At this time, Berniece and Hank had been married thirteen years, five months, and ten days.

Later, Bob would not remember how he came to be at the hospital. He did remember being in the hospital when Berniece entered the emergency room. As Berniece entered the emergency room, she was thinking that Henry had been involved in a bicycle accident, not a motorcycle accident. Berniece was distraught, frantically searching for her son. With all the commotion of trying to meet Henry's medical needs, no one noticed that Bob had been injured in the accident. Bob had an injured ankle and trauma to his neck. The adrenaline was shutting out the pain, but the next day he stiffened up and realized he had been injured. To this day, Bob is plagued with reoccurring neck injuries.

The emergency rescue workers told Henry's parents that he had a head injury and was not expected to live through the trip to Des Moines, Iowa, but they were going to transfer Henry to the Methodist Hospital in Des Moines anyway. Hank insisted on going in the ambulance with Henry to Des Moines. Some friends followed the ambulance. Berniece was driven home to break the terrible news to their daughters that Henry had been in an accident and might die. Berniece sat with the girls and they all cried. Then they prayed together. After this, Berniece took Sherri, Vicki, and Cindi to the Johnstons' home. The Johnstons had their children watch the girls and then they drove Berniece to Des Moines. Berniece would not return home for several weeks.

Freddy Fender was a Spanish singer who sang a song titled "Before the Next Teardrop Falls." That was Henry and Berniece's song. On the way to wrestling practice they would frequently hear this song. Henry was always trying to figure out the parts of the song that were in Spanish. Berniece would not tell Henry that the Spanish part of the song were the same words that were then repeated in English. She would always kid Henry to listen harder. Henry would say, "What is he saying, Mom?" As the Johnstons were driving Berniece to the hospital in Des Moines, the song came on the radio. Berniece began to cry. Mary Johnston asked, "Are you going to be all right?"

Berniece replied, "That's our song."

When Berniece and the Johnstons arrived at the hospital, Henry was still alive, which surprised everybody. Henry was put in pediatric intensive care. He was in a coma and would remain this way for six and a half weeks. There was absolutely no response when they pricked his heels with needles.

In the first forty-eight hours, Henry's condition continued to deteriorate. Henry was bleeding internally. The doctors were unable to determine where the bleeding was originating. A neurosurgeon was called in to assess Henry's injuries. Dr. Hanes found a hairline fracture across Henry's cranium, just over his eyes.

Because of the fracture, the hospital staff stopped all IV and tube feedings until they could stop the bleeding and control the swelling.

This took about two weeks. During this time Henry received the bare minimum for feedings.

Once the swelling went down, the nurses encouraged Hank and Berniece to touch Henry a lot. In addition, they talked and read to Henry. The hospital staff felt this might help bring Henry out of the coma.

The doctors encouraged the family to be supportive by making Henry's hospital room look like his bedroom at home. They were especially encouraged to use visual cues that might help Henry feel he was in a friendly environment. Hank and Berniece arranged Henry's room with objects that had special meaning to him. Henry's room was soon adorned with his football helmet collection, medals, tournament posters, and other items related to wrestling. Since the Seilers were Catholic, they also brought crucifixes into the hospital room, including a crucifix that had been in Henry's room at home. This crucifix was placed on the wall where Henry would be able to see it when he opened his eyes. They hoped that all these things would help Henry to be less overwhelmed when he came out of the coma.

There was no whistle to start this match, just stiff-willed, obstinate pursuit of a self-set goal that can only be judged as Awesome!

5

Dark Night of the Soul

The left side of Henry's head received the impact of the collision with the guy-wire. This is the side of the brain that controls the right side of the body. Swelling also went into the medulla, the structure just above the spinal cord. The medulla is often regarded as an enlarged, elaborated extension of the spinal cord that is contained within the skull. The medulla controls a number of vital reflexes, such as breathing, heart rate, vomiting, salivation, coughing, and sneezing. Damage to the medulla is frequently fatal. The doctors told Hank and Berniece they wouldn't be able to make a prognosis until the swelling in Henry's brain went down.

Henry was in a coma. People often think this is like being asleep; however, Henry's coma paralyzed his body and affected his facial muscles. In young children, the most common cause of brain injury is a sharp blow to the head. This is usually the result of a fall, automobile or motorcycle accident, violent assault, or other trauma. In the United States, about eight million people a year receive such closed-head injuries. Approximately four hundred thousand of them suffer a coma and probable brain damage. Head injuries cause damage by subjecting the brain to rotational forces that drive the brain tissue against the inside of the skull. The inner surface of the skull is quite rough. When there is a blow to the head, the brain is forced to impact the opposite side of the skull. Following the blow, the brain rebounds to the side of the skull receiving the blow. This movement of the brain is called "coup and counter-coup." When the brain tissue moves back and forth, the rough texture of the skull causes further damage to the brain.

When Hank and Berniece entered Henry's hospital room, Henry's face and eyes were swollen due to the head injury. There were black and blue bruises on his face, arms, and legs. His right arm was bent at the elbow, with his right hand tucked under his chin. The two smallest fingers were extended out straight. Henry's left leg had a cut on it, leaving permanent scars. Amazingly, that was the only cut, and there were no broken bones.

On Henry's left arm was a sticker that read, "99% Fat Free." Berniece peeled the sticker off the arm. Henry had been cutting weight to get into a lower weight class in wrestling. The family used motivational stickers to encourage Henry to keep striving for his goals. The day before the accident, Henry had bought a pack of stickers that read "99% Fat Free." Henry had placed one of the stickers on his left arm. This sticker was a painful reminder that just moments ago, Henry had been a vivacious youth with a God-given talent for wrestling.

The boy lay asleep and motionless in his hospital bed. His legs and torso were covered by a sheet and a light brown blanket. Several tubes led from a medical device into his nose and his mouth. Suspended from a rod that rose from the right bed frame corner was a glass bottle. The bottle was inverted so the neck was at the bottom. It had a tube from it that led to his left hand. The tube had pieces of tape about three inches long securing it to a needle imbedded into his hand. The boy, in his unconscious state, had a tendency to pull at his feeding tube. As a result, the boy's left arm was tethered to the side of the bed so it would not move and possibly cause the boy pain in case he turned in his sleep.

The boy's left eye was bulging beneath its eyelid, which now failed to cover the whole eye. The bulging eye was surrounded by a swollen and bruised forehead and temple area. Below the eye, the cheekbone and most of his left cheek was reddish and blue. His nose was disfigured due to the swelling of his cheek. This evidence of a severe blow to the left part of his head was obvious, stealing their attention from his twitching left leg and arm. This twitching motion was sporadic. His left ear was swollen and appeared very sore, as if it had been scraped or punched during the blow to his head.

His breathing was slight, not labored, and he made no other moves besides the periodic twitching. He did not make any facial movements, as some boys do when dreaming.

The boy lay there in this state for days, not waking up. Medical experts bathed him daily and moved him so that bedsores would not endanger his health.

The days turned into weeks. Only once in a long while did he move his head from one side to the other. He seemed very patient as he remained comatose—in a deep, healing sleep.

The youngster had no control of his bodily functions. The food that fed through the tubes digested as it should, but he had no control of his bowels, a conscious and controlled muscle tension. Having lost those faculties, he wore a diaper. Nurse's aides changed the soiled ones whenever necessary.

The right side of his body never moved at all. When bathed or moved, that side stayed stiff, like a flexed muscle. He seemed to have some muscle use on the left side, which at least showed a bit of rigidity when manipulated. There were uncomfortable tremors in the left arm, which the boy would have to deal with the rest of his life.

The boy's right arm and hand gradually atrophied. They began to curl as the muscles contracted. Steps were taken to prevent irreversible atrophy: his arm and hand were massaged and gently straightened out manually to keep it from its curling again. His arm was tied to the bed rail for fifteen minutes every hour to prevent any more curling. The boy often lay with both arms tied to the sides of the bed—the left to keep him from unconsciously ripping out the tubes, the right to prevent the arm from atrophying. Lamb's wool was used on the left side of the boy's head to prevent bedsores from forming. This was needed due to an unconscious thrashing movement.

The parents stared, unbelieving that this was all happening to their only son.

The boy's parents had been given grim news: if he awakened at all, he might not have any conscious brain function. He might have to be institutionalized. His health care would have to be constantly monitored. And if he should be fortunate enough to regain consciousness, his right side would remain paralyzed. The consequences, including life confined to a wheelchair, were staggering. Hank and Berniece's response was, "Well, we'll be there for him no matter what."

There was not a lot the parents of this once spry boy could do but pray. The doctors did encourage the family to take the comatose boy, by wheelchair, outdoors. The reason for these little adventures was to provide the boy with some sensory input. The doctors felt that touching the boy's feet to the soft cool grass and allowing the sunshine to caress his skin could help bring him out of the coma. So, with hope in hand, the family would wheel the boy outside and place his feet on the grass, with the sun shining upon them.

As Henry's body and mind tried desperately to mend, the members of the Marshalltown Wrestling Club were called to action. The club founders organized a "Take Down-a-thon." This fundraiser required the wrestlers to get community members to sponsor them for each takedown they acquired during the competition. This event took place on a Saturday morning at the local Catholic School Gym. Henry's buddy, Steve, and another friend, Jason, were tied for the most takedowns during this event—sixty each. The club raised $11,000, which went to the Henry Seiler Fund.

Henry's fifth-grade class sent an abundance of get well cards. Here are a few of the messages that encouraged Henry's family to keep going.

Henry, I heard you got in a bad motorcycle wreck. That sounds bad. You are a really nice boy and a good wrestler too. I hope you get well soon.

Mindy T.

Henry, we have had so much fun this year. I have finished your art project for you since you are in the hospital. I hope you get better soon.

Your friend, Kyle S.

I hope you get better really quick so I don't have to write a stupid letter like this anymore.

Kevin W.

Hi Henry, I never told you this until now. I hope you get better soon. I think you are a cute boy. Hope you get feeling better and come back to school soon.

Pattie S.

We are hard-pressed on every side, yet not crushed; we are perplexed, but not in despair; persecuted, but not forsaken; struck down, but not destroyed.

II Corinthians 4:8–9

AAU WRESTLERS — Four Marshalltown Wrestling Club members, Dennis Leavy (left), Henry Seiler (middle), Mike Fox (right) and Greg Kearney (standing) have qualified for the Iowa AAU Junior Olympic Freestyle wrestling team. The Iowa team is to wrestle the Mexican Federation team at Cedar Falls High School in a dual meet Tuesday (Tonight) (Staff Photo by Larry Mendenhall)

Four Locals On AAU Mat Team

Four local boys representing the Marshalltown Wrestling Club have qualified for the Iowa AAU Olympic Freestyle wrestling team.

The Iowa team is slated to meet the Mexican Federation team Tuesday night (tonight) at the Cedar Falls High School gymnasium in a dual meet.

The Marshalltown boys wrestling will be Henry Seiler (62 pounds) of Franklin Elementary, Mike Fox (83.5) of Lenihan Junior High, Dennis Leavy (92.5) of Anson Junior High and Greg Kearney (109) of Lenihan.

Three other Marshalltown youths qualified for the Iowa team, but will not be participating because of itinerary and weight/age changes made by the Mexican team. They are Kirk Baker of Hoglan Elementary, Jim Fox of Fisher Elementary and Todd Farrell of Marshalltown High School.

In all, 18 boys qualified to meet the traveling Mexican National team which is a beginning of younger international competition in freestyle wrestling.

Dan Gable, Olympic gold medal winner and assistant coach at the University of Iowa, will officiate the international contest.

The Iowa wrestlers have been holding practices at the University of Northern Iowa under the direction of Ron Mehlin and Mike Ott of Cedar Falls.

Christmas 1972, age 8

School Picture, Age 13, 7th Grade

All Star Baseball Team, 4th grade

Boy Critical After Cycle Crash In City

Officials at Blank Memorial Hospital in Des Moines as of 9 a.m. Thursday reported a 10-year-old Marshalltown boy is in critical condition with head injuries following a motorcycle accident near the Iowa Soldiers Home Wednesday evening.

Police officers said Henry Seiler Jr., son of Mr. and Mrs. Henry Seiler Sr., was injured when thrown from a motorcycle on which he was a passenger. Officers said the driver of the vehicle was Robert R. Logan, 1302 W. Main St., age 16. They said the vehicle went out of control in the 9th and Jerome Streets area sliding over the curb onto a terrace at the east end of the Soldiers Home property and striking a utility pole. Both Logan and young Seiler were taken to Marshalltown Community Hospital East where Logan was treated and released. The Seiler boy was transferred to the Des Moines Hospital a short time later.

Police charged Logan with failing to have control and violating a restricted license. Damage to the vehicle was set at $150. The mishap occurred shortly before 6 p.m.

Police also checked two other incidents Wednesday, one where some $500 damage resulted to a car driven by Michael L. Frye, 1403 S. 4th St., and $250 loss to another driven by Franklin R. Dunham, 505 Roberts Terrace, when the two collided in the Center and Boone Streets area Wednesday at 2:19 p.m.

Some $309 damage was done when a car owned by Frank D. Boriskey Jr., 107½ W. Grant St., rolled free from its parking spot and struck a gas pump at Pester Derby, Monday at 7:15 p.m. No damage other than to the car was caused, records indicate.

Dennis, Henry, Steve - Hunting Trip after
accident - 6th grade

Henry (bottom left hand corner) Junior Varsity,
7th Grade

Seiler family's move to Mason City, IA, Henry age 5

Local Wrestling Club Honors Banquet Held

The Marshalltown Wrestling Club concluded a successful season Thursday night with a banquet and ceremony at the Knights of Columbus Hall put on by the parents of the wrestlers.

Club members, in eight meets, wrestled a total of 981 matches and won 671 while losing 310, a 69 per cent winning record.

The most successful meets for the club were the Pella Little Kids Invitational and the Marshalltown Invitational where the wrestlers compiled won-loss records of 117-32 and 121-49, respectively.

At the banquet, guest speaker Phil Herring, Marshalltown High School wrestling coach, spoke on the value of participation and the future of wrestling in Marshalltown.

The club directors and coaches, Mike Kremer, Larry Fox, Gary Hansen and Tom Crandall, were recognized for their work in getting the club started and coaching the wrestlers. They were presented gift certificates by the club members.

Each wrestler, ranging from grades fourth through eight, was presented a certificate of recognition of outstanding participation and a photostat copy of all articles published concerning the club.

During the course of the season, the Marshalltown Wrestling Club had 43 first places, 47 second places, 29 thirds and 3 fourths. Out of the 100 kids participating, 74 went to tournaments and 55 placed in the top four at least once.

No individual wrestler was recognized as the club doesn't like to place too much emphasis on winning records more than they do participating.

"The kids know when they've done well with the trophies they take home," Kremer added.

The Marshalltown Wrestling Club will be around next year, starting about Christmas time. All four directors plan to return.

MARSHALLTOWN WRESTLING CLUB members, in their first season, accumulated these trophies and medals that were presented to them in an awards banquet and ceremony planned by their parents Thursday night. Of the 100 club members, 75 per cent of them won either a medal or a trophy. (Staff Photo by Larry Mendenhall)

6

The Awakening

As Henry lay in a coma, his family and friends diligently keep watch with the hope of witnessing a miracle. Even after forty-five days, no one gave up hope.

One day, Hank and Berniece were standing at the foot of Henry's bed while wrestling coach, Mike Kremer, was talking to Henry. Mr. Kraemer, as others, had been encouraged to speak to the boy and to use as much sensory language as possible.

Coach Mike held each of Henry's hands in his hands and said, "I can't wait for you to get into position again, Henry. Pretty soon you'll be on that mat again just waitin' for that ref's whistle to go. You can just imagine your muscles all rearin' to push and straining just the right way to get you the victory! You can hardly wait for the ref to slap his hand on the mat as you pin your opponent in record time!"

Henry's hands squeezed the coach's hands, and his forearms became tense. Mr. Kremer visibly jerked in astonishment. Henry's parents jumped to their feet! One scrambled to alert a nurse a few feet outside the doorway. The nurse called for assistance and rushed to the boy's side. Two nurse's aides and a doctor charged into the room.

The medical professionals checked Henry's pulse, blood pressure, and several vital cursory life signs as Hank, Berniece, and Coach Mike clutched each other's hands, trying to stay out of the way but remain in constant view of the still-bruised and sore-looking boy. They begin to cry. But these were sobs of hope. They had just witnessed the resurrection of a life so precious to them that it defied definition.

Henry might just make it! The room resounded with the deafening scream of, "*Yes*! He *is* going to make it! He lives!"

The Seilers—Hank, Berniece, Sherri, Vicki, and Cindi—had not seen Henry conscious since the morning of the accident, forty-five grueling days earlier. The family and friends had wept and waited with anticipation for Henry to pull through.

When Henry started waking up, he would look at his mom and dad and quickly turn away if they would make eye contact with him. At times Henry would look at the people in his room with a blank stare. Berniece felt that Henry was trying to figure out who they were or maybe that his mind was trying to come back to reality. Henry couldn't talk for some time after he awoke. Berniece asked the doctor how long it would be before Henry would be able to talk. The doctor informed Berniece that Henry would be chatting like a magpie before too long.

When staff tried to transfer Henry from his hospital bed to the wheelchair and family members were not present, Henry tended to resist the staff's efforts. One day, a female nurse's aide, named Vietta, tried to get Henry out of bed. Henry was unable to say Vietta, so he referred to her as Velveeta. As Vietta reached across Henry's body, her arm rested against Henry's face, and he bit her. It was clear that Henry needed to learn a form of communication.

The first day of speech therapy was hard. Henry didn't know why he was there and the therapists were all strange to him. It was a long, grueling time from that point on with speech, physical therapy, and occupational therapy. Speech went better than the other two because of Henry's weakened condition. The physical therapy could be grueling. Henry never gave up and the therapists would push him hard.

Therapy was a very difficult part of Henry's recovery. Professionals would make requests of young Henry that involved Henry attempting to walk, talk, and function in his environment. There were times when Berniece wanted to scream, "Leave my son alone; he has been through enough!" Berniece just wanted to take her son home and get life back to normal. But she did not give into this desire; rather, she joined her son in his most challenging match ever—the fight to get better.

Speech therapy mainly involved mouthing words and sounds, breathing exercises, and working from the diaphragm. It seemed like forever before Henry could speak well. Actually, it was only a couple of weeks, but it just seemed like a lifetime. Henry's first words were "Just a little bit." These words were the response to Berniece's question, "Do you like your wrestling buddy, Steve?"

Henry's first weekend home filled the family with joy and trepidation. There was an overwhelming sense of joy, because Henry was finally coming home. There was also fear, because Henry could not walk or talk. Berniece slept at Henry's bedside and would check on him frequently throughout the night.

One morning, Berniece woke to see Henry lying there waiting for her to wake up. As she opened her eyes, she saw that Henry had a smile for her. This affectionate gesture moved her, but it broke her heart to think that Henry could not call out, "Mom, I need you!" or just, "Hi, Mom!" Moms have to have patience, and Berniece had an abundance of patience for her young son.

When Henry was home on the weekends, he refused to stay in his wheelchair. Henry wanted to move about the house without the limitations of a chair with wheels, so when Henry wanted to get from room to room in the house, he would wiggle his way out of the wheelchair, landing gently on the floor. Once he was on the floor, Henry would pull his body across the floor with his left arm. He looked like a caterpillar meandering along a branch on a tree. This gave Henry a sense of freedom and independence. Even at this early stage of recovery, Henry demonstrated the will and perseverance of a champion, the characteristics necessary to make a full recovery.

During these weekend home visits, Henry always had visitors. Ty and Bob would push Henry around the block in his wheelchair. On one such occasion, this threesome was cruising around the block, laughing and telling jokes, when they hit a bump in the sidewalk, one of those cracks in the cement caused by the ever-changing weather of Iowa. The impact almost threw Henry out of the wheel-chair. With arms and legs flailing, the wheelchair was air bound. Bob lunged towards Henry. With arms crossing over Henry's shoulders, Bob managed to keep Henry in the chair. After a second the wheel-chair and its passenger landed safely on the ground.

Slowly, after a couple of weeks, Henry was able to talk with a lot of effort. Before he could talk, though, the sign was one finger for "yes" and two for "no." Finger movement was also labored because of muscular weaknesses throughout Henry's body.

At this stage of recovery, Henry was confined to a wheel chair, and he was unable to vocalize his wants and needs. When Henry tried to communicate, he ended up in tears. The family doctor and staff were worried that Henry had more severe brain damage than first thought. Henry frequently pulled up the hospital gown and pointed to his knees. Berniece and the staff would rub ointment on his knees. This just made Henry's crying more intense. They would ask Henry, "Do your knees hurt?" Henry replied by raising two fingers for no. After about thirty minutes of trying to determine what was bothering Henry, Berniece went to the recreation room and brought back a metal board with plastic magnetic letters. Berniece held the board and letters for Henry to spell what he wanted. To everyone's amazement, Henry spelled, "HOME." The room erupted with shouts of joy. This was a big turning point. They now knew that Henry was able to formulate cognitive thoughts.

At this point, the doctors and the physical therapists informed Hank and Berniece that they would need to prepare the home to accommodate Henry's wheelchair. The prognosis was that Henry would not walk again. The remolding would need to entail widening every door, widening the bathroom, and making the bathtub handicap accessible. Henry's bedroom would also need to be moved to the main floor.

At physical therapy, Henry would have to use a wheelchair for mobility. Using a wheelchair was difficult due to the weakness in the right arm. The physical therapists had looked into placing a slip-wheel on the right side of the wheelchair. (A slip-wheel is an aid for people with only one hand.) Initially, they practiced simply getting to a standing position while the wheelchair was facing a handrail. The length of standing time was gradually increased to two minutes. Once the skill of standing was mastered, the physical therapists taught Henry to walk with a walker. Finally, Henry graduated to walking with a quad-cane. He had to grip the quad-cane in his right hand because of the uncontrollable tremors in his left arm.

As Henry relearned how to walk, he started out taking two to three steps. He had a nurse's aide at his side with a transfer belt (used to move a patient from a sitting position to a walker) around his waist. As Henry practiced walking, his mother, a sister, or Steve would push the wheelchair behind him. Henry went from being able to take two to three steps to fifty steps, and gradually he was walking laps down and back on the physical therapy floor.

The commitment to walking did not cease during weekend passes home. Practicing walking became a part of his daily routine. Henry's sisters helped to keep the task of walking a little more interesting. They would help Henry walk to the Slippery Slide in the backyard. A Slippery Slide is a large strip of heavy-duty yellow plastic. On one end there is an attachment for a garden hose. When the water is turned on, the Slippery Slide is inundated with water. Once Henry made it to the slide, he got his reward: he would sit on the slide and his sisters would pull him along. This activity filled the backyard with laughter and an abundance of wet children.

Henry spent the next three to three and a half months of his life in the hospital. With all the grief and anticipation, life for Hank, Berniece, and the girls was grueling. The family adopted a new motto: "We'll be there for him." And they were true to their word.

While Henry was in the hospital recovering, Berniece stayed in a motel in Des Moines. Hank would drive from Marshall Pack to the hospital every night after work. The girls were cared for by Grandma Bridget, Berniece's mother. This was a very hard time for them; they missed their parents and were left with the feeling of helplessness for their brother. While his parents and the hospital staff cared for Henry in the hospital, his sisters had to stay in school. Sherri, Vicki, and Cindi were bombarded with questions regarding Henry. Peers would ask, "Is Henry dead?" "Is he a retard now?" These types of questions were a constant reminder to the girls that their life had been turned upside down. They made it through this challenging time by receiving support and encouragement from their family and close friends.

If you remember, Henry was the first wrestler to be awarded the Traveling Trophy, given to the wrestler who demonstrated the most determination and energy. Henry was to receive the Traveling Trophy for the second time, once again for his determination and for being energetic. However, this time the match was not with an opponent, but with life itself. Henry had faced being in a coma, and he had won.

The Seiler family taught by example. Hank and Berniece had to divide their attention between Henry's recovery and the day-to-day tasks of raising their daughters. Day after day, somehow, everyone's needs were met. The bottom line: it was all about love.

The key to rehabilitation:
Understand that you will make improvements from day one!

7

A Case Study

This case study was written by a nurse who attended one of the physicians throughout Henry's healing process.

Eric Petersen (assumed name for Henry) is an eleven-year-old who was in a motorcycle accident. Eric had not yet completed his fifth year of school. His grades at that time were average. His father is 38 and is a cattle buyer for a packing company. His mother is 36 and a homemaker who does some baby-sitting in her home. The Petersens have been married for 14 years and also have three daughters, ages 13, 9½, and 8.

On May 7, 1975, Eric was involved in a motorcycle accident. Bob, age 16, who had been giving Eric freestyle wrestling instructions, drove by the Petersens' home and stopped to talk to Eric. Eric wanted a ride so Bob agreed to give him one. While turning a corner the cycle went out of control and hit a wire throwing both youths off. From talking with Bob he told me that right before he was thrown off Eric was thrown against him. Bob got up and found Eric unconscious. The doctor's report said that Eric hit a tree or the curb, but Bob thinks Eric hit the gas tank. At the town's hospital the Petersens were told that Eric's chances were very small. He was rushed to Blank, where his chances weren't any better.

After an examination on 5/20/75, Eric was found to be quite restless and he moved his left leg constantly but didn't move his right leg much. The right arm was held rigid and bent at the elbow. The left was splinted with an IV apparatus. The right pupil didn't seem to react to light, but the left one did somewhat. Both were dilated and unseeing. He had a catheter (tube to withdraw fluid from the body) in his bladder. His reflexes were bilaterally hyperactive and there was bilateral positive Babinski.

The diagnosis was craniocerebral trauma (this is when there is damage to the cerebral hemisphere). His disabilities were coma and right hemi paresis (partial loss of motor function). The loss of function is basically in his right arm and leg at this point. And earlier handicap was his inability to speak.

As I said earlier, it was first thought that Eric wouldn't live. When he came out of the coma, the doctors feared there would be brain damage. When this was ruled out the Petersens were told that Eric's right side might be permanently paralyzed. As my study goes on, one will note how this has changed.

Eric didn't appear to have any different reactions to the doctors and nurses than he did with other people who weren't very familiar to him. He would look at them with an expressionless face. This was the same reaction that I got from Eric when I first met him. I couldn't tell if he was happy or sad. It was just a "look."

The physical therapist told me that Eric didn't like therapy at first. He would get very tense and would cry. Now Eric cooperates and follows verbal instructions. He also remembers activities from session to session. His strength and endurance have increased markedly. As of 6/25/75, he could roll on a mat, sit up, and get up from the floor to a standing position with minimal assistance. Eric can now walk up to two hundred yards with standby supervision for balance. The therapist feels that balance is the main problem at the present time, but that it is improving. Eric's therapist feels that his range of motion is normal in all joints except for his right elbow, which lacks full range.

The occupational therapist works with Eric twice a day for coordination activity of the upper extremities. She feels that his gross coordination is fairly good but that he had difficulty catching a large ball. Eric's grasp and release is not normal and needs work. He can throw a ball a short distance but has problems with the release.

The therapist feels that fine motor coordination is Eric's main problem. He has great difficulty writing with either hand. When he first tried writing with a large crayon he could only scribble. The week of the 23rd he attempted a more normal grasp of a pencil and crayon, but he tends to let go of it. He has been standing without aid at the table and uses his hands for support. He has increased his standing time from two minutes to five but then he needs a rest. Eric was given a weekend pass (6/20–6/22) and the therapist remarked that he verbalizes aloud now and his mental alertness has increased.

Eric at this time (6/25), has been working with the speech therapist only a short time, one week. I stated earlier that his speech was a handicap. For quite a while after he came out of his coma Eric didn't talk—he mouthed words, pointed at objects, and tugged at people to obtain information. On approximately June 13, he began to mouth words and by June 17 he was saying a few words (yes, no, and he could say numbers), but this was all done in a whisper. By the 20th, I could hear some vocalization but not much and it was difficult to understand. On Monday the 23rd, he was talking a great deal about his weekend and the words were very clear. His sentences were choppy but understandable. This was after his weekend pass and I feel this helped his vocalization.

The speech therapist said that Eric can vocalize and is capable of fairly good vocalization, but he occasionally uses false vocal chords. She told Eric's mother that he didn't need much therapy but that he needed to generate more power from his abdominal muscles.

Eric was not given an aphasic test (a test to see if there is total or partial loss of power to use or understand words). She added that he didn't display it when he talked. She found his vocabulary and comprehension tests in the normal range. Eric can read and he can understand what he reads. He basically talks about home and his athletic accomplishments.

The social worker reported that the parents were very pleasant and supportive. Mr. Petersen was described as being aloof at times, however the social worker feels that this is to cover his emotional involvement with Eric. Mrs. Petersen told me that Eric is his "dad's boy." I am sure that this has a good deal to do with his attitude.

Eric's general health status is very good. The doctors believe that he would not have lived if he hadn't been in such good health. His good health also helped him to make such good progress in his recovery.

Eric is very much interested in athletics. His main sport is wrestling, in which he has accumulated many trophies. Eric doesn't care for basketball but will play it if a majority wanted to.

Mrs. Petersen described Eric as being very energetic. "He doesn't like to sit." She also said that he prefers to be outside whenever he can. If the weather doesn't allow for outside activity, Eric embroiders and paints by number. He is pretty good at these activities. Mrs. Petersen pointed out that his handwriting isn't very good because "it takes too long."

The Petersens seem to have good family relationships and enjoy doing things with one another. Mrs. Petersen told me that Eric doesn't like to be touched or held a lot but his sisters do. I guess you could say he's not the "lovey-dovey" type.

Mrs. Petersen and Eric's two friends, Steve and Bob, all feel that Eric prefers peers to adults for company. From observations I noticed how his friends stimulate him the most towards improvement. I feel that the boys have been a big help to Eric, physically, mentally, socially, and emotionally. They know how far to push him because they have been active together. They do understand that he must start from the bottom and work his way up. They have been very patient with him from the beginning.

Eric is a quiet person until you get to know him. I was told that he is very modest and doesn't like a lot of attention. I observed this on several occasions when I would mention that I'd heard he was a champ. He denied it every time.

The three, his mother and two friends, each gave a similar description of Eric when I spoke with them on an individual basis. He's a silent leader rather than a follower and he is very trusting. You could tell him a secret and you'd know that he'd keep it. He has a good sense of humor and really likes good jokes. He is a listener rather than a talker.

Eric's mother told me he takes great pride in his possessions. He cleans his own room because he doesn't want anyone to mess up his football helmet collection. Bob referred to Eric as the "All American Boy." I wholeheartedly agree.

I explained earlier that Eric is basically interested in sports, especially wrestling. He also enjoys football, swimming, baseball, playing cards, chess, and other games. His main interests in school are history and biography. Mrs. Petersen told me that he does enjoy listening to them (mother and father) tell stories about when they were younger.

From observing and working with Eric in the playroom I found him to be a very open and warm individual. He didn't interact with the other children very much and turned off one boy in particular. Eric told me that he didn't like this boy. Whenever this boy approached him, Eric would pretend he didn't see him and go another way.

I observed Eric from 6/13 to 6/20 of 1975. This was only a week due to my two weeks of head teaching. I wish I could have observed him over a longer period of time.

The only immediate goals I can set for Eric involve his physical and motor development.

He does have some difficulty walking and keeping his balance. He also needs to work on fine motor coordination. He has difficulty in grasping things. It is going to take a while for Eric to fully recover the normal use of his body. He has come a long way, but he realizes he's still got a ways to go.

I feel Eric's family and friends are his greatest assets. They have a very accepting and optimistic attitude about his future. Eric will require encouragement and support and I believe his family and friends will stand by him and yet work with him to strive for independence and self-confidence.

The following is the normal level of development for an eleven-year-old, taken from *The Complete Book of Children's Play*, by Ruth Hartley, Ph.D., and Robert M. Goldenson, Ph.D.

Physically, this is the top age for health, activity, and endurance. Growth is slow and regular while manual dexterity is high. Skill in sports means a great deal to both sexes.

Socially, eleven-year-olds are joiners. They do this to establish themselves outside the home and to gain emotional support from the group.

Emotionally, eleven-year-olds are stable. This is the secure age when fears and worries are at a minimum and desire for independence is gathering force. Intellectually they are reaching out for new information and experiences. Life is a big adventure to them and they are eager to explore all kinds of activities.

Success in sports is the key to self-respect and social acceptance. I can see this in Eric's case because he is good and is marked as a silent leader and not a follower. Large muscle activities satisfy the restless urge to rush about and feel energy translated into action. With Eric being involved in wrestling, I'm sure he's translating a lot of energy into action. Team sports are preferred other than individual because of the gang urge and they feel less conspicuous in groups. Eric does participate in some team sports but with his main interest in wrestling I would say that this does not pertain to him. They put their heart and glory in a game and fight for the team and personally glory. Eleven-year-olds frequently expect too much of themselves and are often discouraged by failure and thrilled by success. I really feel this is strong at every age. Being an athlete myself, I have felt like this since I became interested in sports.

At eleven a child is at his height of vitality and doesn't know fatigue. This is very true in Eric's case; in fact, I believe that it's what pulled him through his accident.

I didn't limit my research to this one book, but due to similar findings in all, I chose to quote from the one book. The other books I read on the development of eleven-year-olds are listed in my bibliography.

I would like to thank Eric, his family, his friends, and various hospital staff members for their help in the information for this case study.

Henry was not a quitter; he pushed himself beyond the therapist's expectations.

8

The Long Walk Home

After three months in the hospital, Henry was finally allowed to go home. At last! He was able to go to his own room again! Henry had a difficult time moving around as he wanted to, like he had before he took that fateful ride. Henry never really noticed how slow he was. He moved around his room carefully. Nothing had changed as he opened dresser drawers and explored his bedroom. It was as if he had not been away at all.

Although Henry had moved home, he still had to do exercises. He had not fully regained the strength in his arms, and the whole right side of his body was still a lot weaker than the left side. Henry's right arm didn't stretch out the way it was supposed to, and the left arm seemed sluggish when stretching it out. At least it wasn't painful to stretch out the arms. The muscles were just slow to move the way they were supposed to. Some muscles expand and some contract whenever you move your arm, and Henry's just weren't working together to make his right arm go where he wanted it to go.

Every day, except for the weekends, Henry would get a ride to Des Moines. His mother or father would always accompany him. As they arrived at the hospital, they would go directly to the physical therapy area, where the therapist always greeted them. Henry's parents always made sure that they were on time for these mid-morning appointments.

Therapy would start out by doing some stretching and sit-ups. At each appointment, the therapist would push Henry a little further each time. They usually pushed Henry further along than he wanted to go. After the exercises, the therapist would always take notes on his progress. Then, the therapist would talk to Henry's parents, telling them that he needed more work. Henry was not a quitter; he pushed himself beyond the therapist's expectations.

After Henry came home he was still in a wheelchair. His time in a wheelchair was short lived, though, for Henry was determined to walk again. Henry would get up every morning, after he could get around by himself, and go to the "weight room" in the basement. This room had homemade weights made out of coffee cans and cement, as well as a variety of mats. Hank had made the cement weights with hooks in them. The cans were attached to a pulley system. Henry used these weights to rebuild the strength in his arms.

At first, Henry really couldn't walk very well. He had to use a walker for support, and even with that he was rather wobbly. The daily exercises involved slow, deep knee bends. This was a really tough exercise. Gradually, Henry's coordination improved and he was able to perform flexing movements a little more quickly. After a few long weeks of gradually getting better, Henry was finally able to get rid of the walker.

Balance, stamina, and perseverance were critical at this time. Henry wanted good results and knew that, just like in wrestling, giving a half-hearted attempted would not cut it. It had to be *all*. Not *all or nothing*, just *all*. Henry was determined and stubborn, two traits that carried Henry through the whole "training" ordeal. Training to be a good wrestler was part of who Henry had been before the accident. Training to be normal again had to be a part of who he was after the accident. Henry would later be proud of that stubbornness and determination. Those natural traits have served him well over his lifetime.

One thing was for sure: Henry needed the speech therapy that he received at the hospital. People could not understand him even though he took his time pronouncing each word deliberately. After the physical therapy at the hospital, Henry had to work with the speech therapist every day. It was tiring and frustrating but essential. With school just around the corner, Henry had to really practice at home. He spent many hours in speech and physical therapy. Henry's parents were supportive throughout the entire recovery process.

Shortly after Henry was released from the hospital, his parents let him spend the night at the Johnstons' home. The next morning while Mary was preparing a breakfast of bacon and eggs, Henry asked a profound question. "Why did this happen to me?"

Mary replied, "Henry, no one knows what turns will come in life, but God kept you around for a reason!"

Reflect on how you can better balance "work, love, and play" in your own life.

9

Coming Home Again

You can never really come home again—it's never the same.

In the autumn, Henry went to school again. Besides the kindergartners and first graders, there were no kids who had not heard about the accident. The buzz around school was, "Henry's back." From Henry's perspective, the faces seemed the same; there were kids that had been in fifth grade with him. Some of the kids weren't friends, just kids who knew Henry and whom Henry knew.

Henry did not pretend to know exactly why, but he saw many people change in many different ways. In the sixth grade, it became painfully clear that Henry was no longer a part of the old gang. That the kids he had considered friends in fifth grade behaved differently around him. Some became mean and spiteful.

CHANGE, not habit is what gets most of us down; habit is the stabilizer of human society, change accounts for its progress.

William Feather

Not only had Henry's peers changed, but so had Henry. Henry was more guarded and slow compared to the spring before. Kids would tease Henry's sisters and refer to Henry as "the retard." Some kids must have thought this behavior was harmless. Sometimes the name-calling was blunt and malicious. They would call Henry a "retard" to his face and tease him. They wanted to hurt Henry with their words, and it worked.

The children in Henry's neighborhood would set Henry up for failure. Henry struggled with trying to be a normal sixth grader, but he wasn't. His speech was slurred, his legs moved slower, and his reaction time was delayed. When Henry was outside playing he would try to keep up with the kids, but they would walk faster, leaving him behind. When they played ball, the kids would throw the ball faster than Henry could respond. This was a very frustrating time. He just wanted to fit in, but his body was still in recovery.

Henry was easy prey on the playground, where the guys would pounce on him. One or another would gather friends around and then circle Henry. Then one would say, "Let's get Henry!" and they would swarm him, knocking him down and pinning him. It would only take one of them to pin him, since Henry was unable to force his muscles to act quickly as he had just a year before. No matter how he struggled, Henry was unable to get up. The boys would shout and laugh as Henry tried to maneuver out of being pinned to the ground. Then, as the bell rang or they got tired of holding Henry down, they would get up and stride away, pressing especially hard on his chest, head, belly, or legs. Henry, alone on the grass or gravel, would get up, straighten out, walk back to the classroom, and act as though nothing had happened.

What could Henry do about these hurtful children? He wasn't going to beat them up. He couldn't. He wasn't even the best wrestler anymore. Henry had become average, if not below average. What a feeling! Henry had gone from the top of the heap to the bottom of the barrel, in sports and in popularity, in just a few months.

Henry did get better and started to gain a little respect. It seems everybody wants a piece of you in a competition when they know you were once pretty good. One particular school wrestling meet, a kid beat him. He fought well and beat Henry fair and square, but in this competition, he seemed to be out to get *Henry*, not merely pin his opponent. He seemed hell bent on getting the better of Henry.

After this match, Hank and the kid's father got into a heated discussion. At one point, Hank let this father know what had happened to Henry. Surprisingly, the kid's dad actually apologized to Hank. Henry ended his sixth-grade wrestling season with six wins and eight losses. Henry didn't care. He knew he was a champion.

In junior high, Henry had few friends. He had made great improvements—his color and agility were back—but there was one remnant of the brain injury that he could not overcome: the right side of Henry's mouth wouldn't move when he talked. It was noticeable when Henry answered questions in class.

Henry would forget that he had this little problem. Then he would realize he was slurring his words or speaking unclearly, and he would stop talking. Kids would turn around and look at him. Sometimes these jeers came in a slow, sly way. Other times there was no hesitation in gawking at Henry; they turned around or stretched their heads towards Henry to see what was making him talk funny. It wasn't funny. Henry often felt bad and wanted to strike out at others, but this was Henry's struggle, no one else's! Henry had a lot of healing to do.

If you see Henry in pictures taken around that time of his life, you will see a droop to the right side of the mouth. Henry tried to strengthen those muscles so his mouth wouldn't droop, but it took a long time to get that back to normal. Thanks to a lot of therapy and work, Henry came out of it. At this time, Henry was also plagued with violent headaches, frequently triggered by exposure to light. These intense headaches lasted for one year.

Despite all of the shortcomings of Henry's recovering body, he still participated in wrestling. It was difficult for Henry to go from a champion wrestler to an average to below-average wrestler. During seventh grade, Henry only qualified for the junior varsity team and in eighth and ninth grade he made the varsity team.

During junior high, Henry remembered that in eighth grade he was unlike his peers in another way, too. Boys his age developed pubic hair, underarm hair, and hair on their legs. Henry's case was different. The brain damage occurred mostly on the left side of brain, so the right side of his body was affected. Henry actually had no hair on the right side of his body.

Doctors ran tests. Hank and Berniece were very concerned about this lack of hair growth. Their son had hair in the regular places that a boy his age would have hair, but only on the left side of his body. Henry was just plain embarrassed. Going into the locker room at school to get dressed for phys-ed was hard to deal with. Taking his shirt off and exposing his armpits subjected him to unkind comments from others. Henry would become self-conscious and then they would sense his discomfort, so they would take special notice. These boys would frequently chant, "No right armpit hair and no right leg hair. What else has no hair? How about the pubic area?"

Henry never let the kids prove it one way or the other. At school, they had four or five showers all in a row without walls between them. Sure enough, there was always one kid who just had to peek.

Henry tried to keep himself respectful and tried to keep prying eyes from finding out about his private parts. The truth was that Henry did indeed lack hair on the right side of his groin area.

Hank and Berniece were very concerned about this lack of hair growth. The doctor ran many tests and said that Henry's hair would grow in time. The doctor was right. It was just a matter of time, as he said. It was all but forgotten within about six or nine months.

In the ninth grade, Henry was starting to feel at peace with himself after going through so much relating to his accident. As junior high progressed, Henry gained a few more friends. He became use to the new school, also. Henry's life seemed to be getting back on track.

Henry received a lot of support from his dad. Hank made sure they did as much stuff together as they could. Hank would take Henry hunting. Henry would joke that he was like a bird dog to his dad. Henry would get the pheasants he shot. Then he would dress them and the family loved to eat them.

Fishing was also a lot of fun. Hank and Berniece would take Henry to lakes and streams not too far from Marshalltown. They taught Henry how to bait the hooks, set the bobbers, cast, and make sure the fish didn't just eat the bait, but really bit into the hook. They didn't always come home with a lot of fish, but they *did* come home with common experiences. Hank and Henry did a lot together. Henry feels this was a smart thing his dad did, keeping Henry close to him like that. Henry and Hank have great memories. During these times together, Hank was able to teach Henry some of his principles of life.

During the fall of 1974, Hank took Henry deer hunting in Nebraska during bow season. They were accompanied by Steve Dunn, Henry's friend, and his father, Frank Dunn. This was a great time for Henry and Steve to learn about hunting safety, tracking, and the thrill of the hunt.

The fall after the accident, Hank took Henry deer hunting again. This time Dennis Leavy (son of Frank and Eilenn Leavy) and Bernie Johnston (son of Palmer and Mary Johnston) went along for the hunt. Henry's parents, with all their close friends and extended family, tried to keep life as normal and enjoyable as they could considering all the changes that the Seiler family had endured.

All the while Henry was in the hospital, either Hank or Berniece was at his side. Berniece was there most of the time. That is because Hank had a job to do. He couldn't just stop earning money. There were many expenses to deal with. There were wonderful people who helped Berniece and Hank take care of his sisters so Berniece could tend to Henry. These wonderful individuals did not expect it and might not have received a satisfactory "Thank you!" The family had many dear friends who empathized and acted on that quality in their lives. These friends provided support in some capacity, if not in many capacities. Thanks to all!

During this time in Henry's life, Hank provided for the family by buying cattle for Marshall Pack.

Sometimes Hank took Henry with him to the cattle auctions, where he bought cattle for the beef producers. Henry remembers the drive to the auction house. He remembers the smells around the auction house. Some of those smells contradicted one another! For example, there was the smell of hay and manure around the holding pens, and the contrasting smell of the coffee and pies and doughnuts at the auction house café.

When Henry was in eighth grade Hank rented acreage in the country, where they could take some of the bargains Hank would buy at the sale barn. Hank would show Henry what to look for and explain why it was a good buy. Sure enough, Hank and Henry brought calves of varying sizes to "the farm" and the children would do the chores. Sometimes Henry did the chores alone, making sure the animals had plenty of water. Henry enjoyed getting them plenty of hay to eat and making sure their sleeping quarters were clean. When it was cold, they were given a warm place to sleep. After the cattle were big enough to sell for a profit, Hank would sell them. Sometimes, they had sheep or pigs to raise. Henry's sisters had horses that they enjoyed riding. The family even had ducks around "the farm" that Berniece and Hank would butcher. The ducks were roasted and prepared for dinner by Berniece.

Throughout all of this, Hank let Henry earn money by doing chores and sharing the money from the sale of the livestock. In addition, at the age of thirteen, Hank obtained a job for Henry at the Marshall Packing Company cleaning offices. There was always a lesson to learn when Henry was by Hank's side. Hank taught Henry by example and by showing him what a dollar was worth. God bless him for that! Henry carried these lessons with him all of his life, and the value of a dollar made sense to him.

But one thing I do, forgetting those things which are behind and reaching forward to those things which are ahead, I press toward the goal for the prize of the upward call of God.
Philippians 3:13–14

10

Adult Life

Throughout Henry's high school years, he struggled to develop his academic skills. Henry attended a three-week vocational rehabilitation training course. Afterwards, he was tested and then trained to do state-funded jobs (e.g., laundry) at a state institution. Later, Henry was employed by the Veterans Home in Marshalltown, Iowa (where the accident took place). Henry started out part time in dietary. This was not the right job for Henry, so he requested a transfer to housekeeping. He worked in this department for one year. Henry was a quick and thorough cleaner. He would frequently complete a quarter to a third more work than his coworkers. Yet Henry was frequently told, "Your floors aren't clean enough. Go watch the video." Henry became tired of housekeeping.

Henry was labeled as a "mentally slow person" because of his brain injury and vocational training. He was frequently criticized and put down. When frustrated, he would say, "I'm smarter than all of you! You're the ones with an attitude problem." Henry eventually requested a transfer to laundry. He was treated the same way. His boss was an okay guy and assured Henry that he was doing a good job. However, his boss' boss wanted Henry moved out of laundry due to the tension within this department.

These frustrations at the Veterans Home landed Henry at Grinnell College, forty miles south of Marshalltown, Iowa. Henry was enrolled in the Nurse's Aide Program. Henry completed this program and attempted to transfer into nursing at the Veterans Home. The director of nursing would not hire him because of his head injury. At this time, Henry was dating a girl in nursing who was trying to help Henry get into the nursing department. When coworkers gave her trouble about Henry's abilities to handle the stress of the job, Henry would tell them to "lay off!"

The director of nursing commented, "This is the way head-injured people react." Henry had become stereotyped as a "slow person with a head injury." The director of nursing felt that Henry would not be able to handle the pressure of working in the nursing department. Unfortunately, people were unable to see past the label that he had received twelve years earlier. Henry finally received a job as a nurse's aide after filing a complaint with the union. He stayed in this position for five years.

Even though people let the label of "Slow Person with a Head Injury" get in the way, Henry never let this keep him from getting what he wanted to achieve.

At the age of twenty-nine, Henry took on another life challenge. His friend entered him in a 5K race. Henry began a daily training routine. He started out running a half-mile and gradually increased the length of his daily run. Henry took first place in the 5K race for his age group, running a 7.20-mile average. One month later, Henry was entered into another race. During this 3.85-mile race, Henry took first place for his age group, running a 6.59-mile average.

At the age of thirty-seven, Henry registered a domain for a dot-com site, "2 Pathetic Guys." He is currently creating the 2patheticguys.com site into a franchise and cartoon series.

Even though people let the label of "slow person with a head injury" get in the way, Henry never let this keep him from getting what he wanted to achieve.

11

A Message of Encouragement

The Key to SUCCESS is to never give up at any age!

Henry's message throughout this book is twofold. The first theme is *Persevere in your ambitions*. Perseverance involves discipline and a positive attitude. Henry entered into his greatest life challenge with a well-established sense of discipline and positive self-regard. The discipline that he learned in wrestling gave him the extra drive he needed to learn to walk, talk, and dress himself all over again.

The second theme is *Never give up on your kids*. You will likely need the support of friends and loved ones. Henry had the support of his family and close friends. Children are a parent's greatest asset; support them in their dreams and ambitions.

Henry used the same strong-willed determination in life as he did developing his skills in folkstyle and freestyle wrestling. He used this determination to surmount life's physical challenges. He also used it to overcome the emotional rollercoaster that his life became.

"We'll be there for our child no matter what."

Henry's personal motto is,

"I know where I am going and I know what it takes to get there."

Rarely did Henry have an actual tangible goal, but he always kept this motto close to his heart. This ended up being his formula for success.

Henry knows what it is like to be flat on his back, staring at the ceiling tile, but he made a great reversal and came out a winner!

Cheryl Seiler, Henry's aunt

Appendix A

Reflections from Family and Friends

Sherri (Henry's sister)

I know that this was the hardest thing our family has ever dealt with, but Henry's determination to get better prevailed. He is now a very independent person and has made a full recovery. I will add that he never missed a year of school because of this—he was able to graduate with his class. We are all very proud of Henry and all his accomplishments. Most of all, we are proud to call him our brother and the best uncle to my children.

Bob Logan (Henry's best friend)

When I was a junior on the Marshalltown High School wrestling team, I began assisting a club training at a local grade school. Among other things, the champions in that group were training for a meet with a touring Mexican Team. Several of those, including Henry, continued training with me on a mat I had installed in my parents' basement for that particular event.

I remember that Henry was strong and liked the headlock or "head and arm" as it is called variously across the country. With this technique, Henry could take an opponent from his feet or knees right to his back and pin him. It is a showcase maneuver in wrestling, a real crowd pleaser.

Life seemed exciting to us in our little corner of the world. We were looking forward to challenges and working hard to achieve our success. Everyone around us was excited for us. Henry had won this particular bout. It seemed we were relishing the moment, looking for the next mountain to climb. As it turns out, the next mountain was the aftermath of the accident.

Henry's parents, his mother in particular, were dedicated parents and boosters for their child's interests. So, we had all the ingredients for success in life at this point: Henry was already a kid who could get off his butt, live hard, and go for it—not just do enough to get by. He was in outstanding physical condition, mentally though, and used to success. He had loving and supportive parents.

He was quiet, like his father, but he had a steely resolve to win. He did not like getting taken down. His style was not to move and sting like a bee but to grind down and crush. There were quicker opponents, but they could not quite get the drop on him. In the end, it comes down to resolve.

In retrospect, Henry's recovery was characteristic of him.

Noreen Kelly (Henry's aunt)

In May 1975, my mother called to tell me that my nephew, Henry Seiler, had been injured in a motorcycle accident. He had been taken to a hospital in Des Moines, and his injuries were serious.

I asked how it happened, but she didn't know. I asked if his parents were with him, and I asked about his sisters, but she didn't have any more information. My mother said she would let me know when she had more details. She was trying to keep from crying, and I felt so sorry for her.

When we talked again, Mother told me that Henry was in a coma and his parents were with him in the hospital. She also told me that she was going to their home to take care of his sisters.

It was several weeks before he came out of the coma, and then the long recovery and rehabilitation began. Henry's patience and persistence have helped him make a remarkable recovery.

Cheryl Seiler (Henry's aunt)

I remember receiving the call as if it were yesterday. Henry had been in a motorcycle accident and was in a coma. I was full of shock, disbelief, and sadness—and how would I tell my children? The hard part was being so far away. I wanted to be there right now. Not only were we related, but Berniece (Henry's mom) was my best friend, even before we married brothers. Berniece was a strong person, but, I thought, was she strong enough to deal with what lay ahead of her and the family? After a few days of Henry not improving and receiving word he was still in a coma, we began to make arrangements to leave the children with my mom. We needed to be there, especially when Hank (Henry's dad) said, "I'm really worried about Berniece." At that time, she hadn't left the hospital. She wasn't sleeping or eating. It was time to go.

I remember arriving at the Children's Hospital in Des Moines and thinking back to when we went there when Henry was an infant. He was there with his parents to check on the reasons for his convulsions. If I remember correctly, it was due to the formula he was on.

I remember walking in and Hank sitting all alone in the lobby. Berniece was in the room with Henry. I remember being told that when we went into Henry's room, we needed a positive attitude. No tears, no negative remarks, only positive talk. It was hard, but we did it.

I remember seeing our little Henry, who was such an active boy, lying so lifeless. All he was wearing was his underwear. One time, a young guy came in and did exercises on Henry's arms and legs to keep his muscles strong.

After, a while I finally convinced Berniece to go to the apartment complex they had while they were there. There we cried, talked, and cried. I listened, cried some more, and we shared many things. Finally, she thought she could sleep some, and she did. After a few hours of sleep, Berniece showered and was ready to face the day.

I remember thinking, *She's going to be okay, for the time being.* She was strong and on top of everything, and we both knew Henry was in God's hands and she wasn't ready to send Henry back to him.

We returned to the hospital and it was Mike's turn to get his brother to sleep. I remember sitting in the waiting room all night and seeing all sorts of people come and go. At one time Berniece said, "You know, Cheryl, we're not so bad off. It could be worse. At least Henry's body parts are all intact and there's still hope he'll come out of this. Some of these parents have no hope, only time."

I remember the kids coming for a visit and how bad I felt for Sherri. She had given Henry permission to ride with this kid on the cycle. No one blamed her, especially not her folks. It was an accident, but what a hard thing to learn at such a young age. I think my heart went out to her the most. It was hard to leave them all that day.

When we picked up our children, we couldn't hug them enough. We had bought a mini-bike for the boys, but we sold it the next week. I remember cringing every time I saw someone riding a cycle without a helmet. They didn't realize how a split-second fall could affect their lives and those of so many loved ones around them.

After we were home for a while, Henry was still in a coma. We were sitting on our front porch when the family priest stopped to visit. He knew about the family crisis and wanted to know how we were doing and to get an update on Henry. When we told him Henry was still in a coma, his response was, "I think it's time to turn this over to William." William was a very special person, a patient at Willmar Regional Treatment Center, where Father was a counselor. Father had more or less adopted William, who was Mass server for all of Father's Masses at the hospital. We had never heard of William before this. We attended Mass out there to meet William. He was a special person and very dedicated to God. He was praying for Henry and told us he would continue to pray until we told him that Henry was better. It was never *if* he gets better but *when* he gets better.

A few weeks later, we received word that Henry had come out the coma. How excited we were! We were told that Henry still had a long road ahead of him, but we knew he would make it. With his family's love and determination, William's prayers, and ours, Henry would make it. What a joy it was the day Henry and his family came here to thank William personally.

Since that time, William has passed on, but our family still considers him the closest thing to a saint we have known.

We had another nephew who at the age of twenty-three was diagnosed with cancer. William prayed for him too. Both our nephews are alive today!

Henry is one special person, and God let us have him with us instead of taking him home. One more thought, as I look back. Henry and his family were very much involved in the sport of wrestling. Henry was good! He had the potential to be one of Iowa's great wrestlers. We were sad when he couldn't wrestle anymore, but as the years passed, we realized that Henry *is* one of Iowa's great wrestlers, only in a different way. He knows what it is like to be flat on his back, staring at the ceiling tile, and then make a great reversal and come out a winner!

ppendix B

APPENDIX B

TAKE DOWN-A-THON

Henry J. Seiler Trust Fund

The following is a list of wrestling participants and the amount of money each wrestler raised during the **TAKE DOWN-A-THON:**

Arch Allison, age 12, $94.00

Mike Allison, age 10, $20.00

Jeff Arnold, age 10, $58.00

Dan Arnold, age 12, $58.00

Kirk Baker, age 13, $105.00

Tom Barten, age 13, $50.00

Doug Beals, age 13, $25.00

Steve Booth, age 15, $100.00

Rick L. Carter, age 14, $17.00

Todd Chambers, age 10, $35.00

Mark Cohen, age 11, $55.45

Tom Condie, age 13, $20.00

Steve Dunn, age 12, $166.26

Danny Evans, age 11, $174.00

Dave Evans, age 12, $75.00

Bill Ficken, age 15, $20.00

Ed Ficken, age 16, $30.00

Jim Fox, age 11, $39.00

Mike Fox, age 13, $41.00

Wade Gossett, age 16, $40.00

Mike Harms, age 15, $65.00

Jimmy Hunt, age 12, $105.00

Mike Jenkins, age 13, $60.00

Craig W. Johnson, age 18, $70.00

Bernie Johnston, age 13, $65.00

Ron Johnston, age 18, $30.00

Greg Kearney, age 13, $20.00

Kelly Kreitlow, age 12, $105.00

Bill Lambert, age 11, $100.00

Dennis Leavy, age 14, $68.00

Todd LeCocq, age 11, $68.25

Tom Lewis, age 17, $99.00

Bob Logan, age 16, $319.00

Brant Luense, age 13, $99.00

John Peter, age 14, $162.00

Brandy R. Ray, age 19, $45.00

Barry Reed, age 11, $40.25

David Reisetter, age 12, $79.25

Rick Relph, age 12, $76.00

Ken Rethmeier, age 14, $115.00

Rich Robeson, age 11, $41.00

Rick Rogers, age 14, $59.50

Jason Roseland, age 9, $20.00

Jay Shiek, age 11, $2.00

Phil Shipley, age 13, $60.00

Dennis Smith, age 16, $5.00

Greg Smith, age 26, $5.00

Mark Sommerlot, age 14, $80.00

Peter Southard, age 14, $80.00

Tom Scott & Lou Swanson, $25.00 (donation)

Kurt Terrillion, age 12, $24.60

Kevin Vaughn, age 12, $70.00

Paul Whitaker, age 13, $5.00

Frank White, age 19, $10.00

Craig Whitehill, age 17, $25.00

Creighton Whitehill, age 11, $25.00

Russ Wiederholt, age 15, $100.00

Wes Wilkinson, age 10, $34.00

John Wolfe, age 11, $80.00

Jay Zier, age 11, $38.00

Thank you for your support!

978-0-595-47861-3
0-595-47861-1

Made in the USA
Middletown, DE
01 December 2014